The ABC□ Photographic Copyright

British Photographers' Liaison Committee

Published by
British Photographers' Liaison Committee
81 Leonard Street, LONDON EC2A 4QS
Tel: 020 7739 6669
Fax: 020 7739 8707

© Copyright Honorary Secretary, British Photographers' Liaison Committee 1999

ISBN 0 9514671 2 3

Legal Notice
This work contains a general statement of the law as of June 1999. It should not be relied on for definitive answers or advice on specific points of law or otherwise. Each case will in practice depend on all its surrounding circumstances, and specific advice should be sought from a legal advisor or a professional association. Whilst every effort has been made to ensure the accuracy of this publication the publishers cannot accept any liability arising out of any of the material contained in this publication.

Publishing history
First published in 1989 as
The Photographers' Guide to the 1988 Copyright Act
Revised and reissued in 1994 as
The ABC of UK Photographic Copyright

Our thanks to:

- **David List, Sal Shuel, Geoffrey Adams, Gwen Thomas, Mike Laye** and **Janet Ibbotson** for all their efforts in the research, writing and compilation of this book.

- **Simon Shuel** for his design skills.

- **Lord Brain** for his campaigning on behalf of photographers.

- Solicitor **Charles Swan** of The Simkins Partnership for his legal advice on the contents of this work.

- The **Journalists' Copyright Fund** for their generous financial support.

- And, finally **Demis Roussos** for his continuing inspiration.

Contents

Introduction

This is The Photographers' Guide to the 1988 Copyright Act - as amended by 'The ABC of UK Photographic Copyright' and now further amended to take in all the changes in copyright law that have occurred since that work was published in 1994. 'As amended' is what is added to Acts of Parliament when sections have been changed. The 'as amended' bits are usually put in because the original Act has been found to have anomalies. In this case the anomalies that are being dealt with are the result of attempts to harmonise the law of copyright across all the states of the European Economic Area and elswhere in the world. The first publication in 1989 was intended to be an 'ABC' of copyright for photographers but because it appeared soon after the Act became law and there was no way of knowing how the Act would affect photographers and their clients, it soon became obvious that it was an 'AB' without the 'C'. The 'ABC' corrected this omission to a certain extent but harmonisation efforts throughout the European Union and European Economic Area changed some of the rules almost as soon as the publication was ready for press. This edition now brings the text fully up to date, even if we have yet to achieve the forecast A-Z of copyright for photographers.

The Committee on Photographic Copyright was formed in 1981 to represent the interests of photographers during the formulation of the new Copyright, Designs and Patents Act. The Committee was particularly concerned with the protection of photographers' work. Though the 1956 Copyright Act recognised photographs as artistic works, they were not protected to the same extent as other artistic works. Extensive lobbying by the Committee, its member Associations and several individual photographers resulted in the wholesale reform of the law on copyright in photographic works in the 1988 Act. Having succeeded in achieving most of what was required, the Committee evolved into the British Photographers' Liaison Committee which continues to represent the interests of all photographers. Inevitably the 1988 Act threw up problems which only emerged as the Act matured. On August 1 1989, the day the Act came into force, the first problem thudded through many photographers' letterboxes in the shape of a £1 coin attached to a document which should be returned, signed, to the advertising agency which had generated it. This agency had read the Act and intended to maintain the situation as it had been previously. A signature assigned copyright in everything done, in perpetuity, to that particular agency. Some signed it without thinking. Some returned the money with the contract with no comment. Some poured out a stream of invective. Some pocketed the money and threw the contract in the bin thereby storing up trouble for themselves. Some approached their professional associations who poured oil on troubled waters and sorted out the problem as well as they could under the circumstances.

'New Technology' meant very little when the Act was written and was dealt with in few words. Now, more than ever, it evolves from day to day, bringing with it problems of copyright management which the drafters of the 1988 Act could not foresee; hence the need for many of the changes. It is a function of the BPLC to monitor this kind of change, absorb as much information as possible and to recycle this to its members in an easily digestible form, thereby enabling both photographers and their clients to be aware of what is involved without coming to blows. It is hoped that with this publication the BPLC continues to fulfil its role as the industry professional practice body.

Members of the British Photographers' Liaison Committee:
The Association of Historical and Fine Art Photographers
The Association of Photographers
The British Association of Picture Libraries and Agencies
British Institute of Professional Photography
Chartered Institute of Journalists
Institute of Medical Illustrators
Master Photographers Association
National Union of Journalists
The Royal Photographic Society

Observers:
Association of Illustrators
The Chartered Society of Designers
The Design and Artists Copyright Society
The Institute of Information Scientists
The Library Association
NAPLIB
National Association of Artists
Picture Research Association (Formerly, Society of Picture Researchers and Editors)

The essentials

What is copyright?
Copyright is a property right vested in works which authors have created. The law of copyright:

Protects against unauthorised reproduction of works; and

entitles copyright owners to economic benefit

whilst seeking a fair balance between the interests of authors and users of copyright materials.

What are moral rights?

The right not to have one's work subjected to derogatory treatment

The right to be identified as the author of one's work

The right not to have a work falsely attributed to oneself as author

Right of privacy for photographs commissioned for private and domestic purposes

Copyright law originally came into being to ensure that individual craftsmen received proper economic compensation for the products of their craftsmanship. The problem for photographers was always that UK law excluded them from first ownership of copyright when work was commissioned and therefore denied them the protection and benefits afforded to composers, illustrators, writers and painters, etc.

Largely because of the lobbying of 19th century portrait painters who felt threatened by the advent of photography, the work of British photographers and engravers became treated as a copying technique and, unless it was agreed otherwise, copyright was vested in the commissioner rather than the author of the work.

This view of photography, apart from being basically unfair, was contrary to legislation in much of the rest of the world and has led to confusion at one time or another for nearly everyone involved, either as creator or user. The implementation of the Copyright, Designs and Patents Act 1988 has done a lot to improve the situation although many people, including photographers themselves, still have to cope with rights in photography generated under legislation going back to 1862, which were left largely intact by the 1988 Act and now also have to deal with the complications produced by the copyright harmonisation measures brought in throughout the European Union and the European Economic Area. (Like the European Union, the European Economic Area is defined by international agreement and may vary over time. Readers needing to know the membership of the EEA are therefore advised to check on the latest position at the time their need arises).

The most important thing to remember about the 1988 Act is that, like Magna Carta, that other great symbol of protest against unjust treatment at the hands of the powerful, it redresses a long term injustice, giving photographers the legal status of authors of their own work, control over the rights in it, how it is used and the right to a credit.

The major points of UK copyright legislation

Authorship

Photographers are now in the same position as all other authors, ie, the person who creates the photograph is the author of it. However this does not apply to employed photographers for work created in the course of their employment and it should also be remembered that 'person' includes the idea of a 'legal person', ie, a company or organisation. This can, and does cause problems when trying to identify the rightful owner of 'extended' or 'revived' copyright. 'Extended' and 'revived' copyright are new terms written into UK law as the result of agreement within the European Union that copyright legislation is economically and culturally important enough to need a common approach across all the member states. In order to achieve this common approach the duration of existing copyright protection periods have been extended and, most unusually, copyright protection periods which have expired have been revived to give a period of protection equivalent to the new minimum standard of 70 years after the death of the author. In parallel with this, the new legislation sets out how to decide ownership since ownership and authorship of copyright often rest in different hands. The detail is discussed below.

Ownership of copyright

In general, the author of the work is the first owner of any copyright in it, so photographers now have the first ownership of copyright in their work whether it was commissioned or not.

Ownership of the new 'extended' copyright is as follows:

The person who was the owner of the copyright immediately before January 1 1996 is the owner of the extended copyright, unless they owned it for less than the full term of copyright, in which case the extended copyright goes to the person entitled to the copyright after the intitial owner's term has expired. This date at the beginning of a year is there simply to give legal certainty to the changes and to avoid the need in the majority of cases to make messy calculations over duration. Nevertheless, specialist legal advice may be needed to clarify ownership when the need arises because the legislation does contain other dates which may be relevant for particular purposes or territories.

Ownership of the new 'revived' copyright is as follows:

The person who was the owner of the copyright immediately before expiry reacquires it. If that person died before January 1 1996 (or, in the case of a legal person such as a company, ceased to exist) the copyright reverts to the author, or the administrator of the author's estate if the author is also dead. The 'author' for these purposes is always the person who created the photograph (notwithstanding different definitions of authorship in the 1911 and 1956 Copyright Acts). If there is no administrator the copyright passes to the UK government.

Specialist legal advice may be needed to clarify the situation because of the changing provisions as to first ownership of copyright since 1862. Copyright frequently belonged under pre-1988 legislation to the owner of the negative or the commissioner of the photograph. Other complications such as bankruptcy, insolvent companies and the like may cloud the issue and will also require such specialist advice if the situation warrants it.

Copyright can be assigned to another person but only if the photographer agrees. An assignment of copyright should be in writing signed by or on behalf of the assignor but a verbal or contractual agreement will often, in practice, be equally effective. Assignments of copyright in all future work created for a client, should not be agreed because this is rarely in the best interests of the photographer. Each commission should be negotiated separately. The circumstances of one job will be different from another. It may be preferable to retain control of material from one session but not from another for the same client.

Employed photographers

Employed photographers do not own copyright in work created 'in the course of their employment' unless they have an agreement to the contrary. A good yardstick for defining 'employed' in the UK is if an employer pays PAYE and National Insurance, but this is not conclusive. Work on a freelance basis does not constitute being 'employed'. Photographers working freelance on a six month contract or a residency will normally be required to sign a contract of employment. They should instead sign a contract for services, preferably one which has been drawn up on professional advice and which deals fairly with the interests of all parties. Ownership of copyright in photographs taken by employed photographers is a grey area and the issue should be properly addressed by employers and employees, both of whom should be clear where they want to stand at the end of this! It should also be remembered that photographers who form themselves into a limited liability company can also be employees and that copyright will belong to the company (and may therefore be lost in the event of receivership or liquidation unless copyright has been retained by the photographer). This issue should be sorted out on the formation of the company, but can be done at any time and should always be done with good legal advice.

Computer-generated works

A new feature in the 1988 Act was the provision from August 1 1989 for 'work that is generated by computer in circumstances such that there is no human author of the work' with copyright expiry 50 years from the end of the calendar year in which the work is made. Having ruled out human authorship and copyright expiry based on the usual author's life plus so many years, by sleight of hand the Act proceeds to say the author of this kind of work is taken to be the 'person by whom the arrangements necessary for the creation of the work are undertaken'; a formula which allows assertion of the moral right against 'false attribution' but excludes the 'integrity' or 'paternity' moral rights for obvious reasons. (See the section on Moral Rights for an explanation of these rights).

This provision has yet to be tested in the courts and would appear to apply mostly to scientific, technical and remote surveillance photography where exposure timing and frequency, focus and tracking, etc, are all computer controlled. It goes without saying that this section of the Act does not create this novel kind of copyright ownership for such things as automatic copying or manipulation of photographs or film, artistic works of all kinds and other works of 'artistic craftsmanship' which of course, may have their own copyright which will require to be cleared before any such copying is undertaken.

Duration of copyright protection from August 1 1989

The duration of copyright in photographs taken on or after August 1 1989 whose country of origin is a European Economic Area state or which are taken by a national of an EEA state is now the same as for all other artistic works - 70 years from the end of the year in which the author dies.

Photographs by a national of a non-EEA state whose country of origin is not an EEA state have a duration which is that granted in their country of origin up to a maximum of life plus 70 years. 'Country of origin' is a new concept which has been introduced to distinguish between EEA originated works and those which are not. 'Country of origin' has a complex definition which can involve determining the author's nationality, or the date of creation of the photograph, or the date and place of first publication in order to arrive at the actual duration of protection. In any event duration in the UK will not exceed life plus 70 years.

For works of joint authorship, the duration of copyright is 70 years from the end of the year of the death of the last surviving author, provided that at least one of the authors was a national of an EEA state or the photograph's country of origin is an EEA state. For other photographs duration is that granted by their 'country of origin' up to a maximum of life plus 70 years.

Again, although this change happened from January 1 1996 in response to the EU copyright harmonisation measures it applies equally to all photographs taken from August 1 1989. The 50 year period of protection introduced by the 1988 Act has been superseded. Apart from photographs subject to Parliament, international organisations or non-EEA copyright there are now no photographs taken in the period August 1 1989 to January 1 1996 to which the 50 year rule applies.

For works taken by unknown photographers duration of copyright is now 70 years from the end of the year in which the photograph was first made available to the public (whether published, exhibited, shown in a film or broadcast) provided this takes place within 70 years from the end of the year in which the photograph was taken. If not made available to the public copyright expires 70 years from the end of the year in which the photograph was taken.

If the photograph carries a pseudonym as credit, or there is no credit at all the author will be considered unknown if actual identity cannot be ascertained by 'reasonable enquiry'.

Photographs which are subject to Crown copyright have different rules. Crown copyright in the UK now lasts for a maximum of 125 years from the end of the year in which the photograph was taken. If the photograph is commercially published within 75 years of the end of the year in which it was taken, copyright lasts for 50 years from the end of the year of publication. In other countries where Crown copyright also exists, eg, Australia, Canada, etc, but its duration is controlled by the legislation of their independent parliaments, duration is still only 50 years from making or publication. When Parliament or certain international organisations (like the UN, Interpol, etc) are the copyright owners, it will usually be for 50 years from the end of the year in which the photograph was taken.

Duration of copyright protection before August 1 1989
It is important to remember that the provisions of the Acts dealing with copyright of 1862, 1911 and 1956 were each carried over by the superseding Act up to the 1988 Act and still apply to photographs taken before the commencement of the 1988 Act on August 1 1989. Add to this the EU harmonisation measures and it will be well into the next century before the cumulative effects become history. The 1911 Act (which came into force on July 1 1912) granted copyright protection in a photograph for 50 years from the end of the year in which the negative was made, replacing the 7 year period of protection for unpublished works or 42 years from date of first publication granted by the 1862 Act. 'Authorship' was placed in the hands of whoever owned the original negative at the time the picture was taken, not necessarily the person who took the photograph. If the photograph was commissioned the copyright belonged to the commissioner unless otherwise agreed.

The 1956 Act (which came into force on June 1 1957) granted copyright protection in a photograph for 50 years from the end of the year of first publication and also gave perpetual copyright to unpublished photographs taken from the commencement of the Act. 'Published' meant (and still does) issuing reproductions of a work to the public. A photograph exhibited in an exhibition was not 'published' but a printed version in the catalogue of the same exhibition would have been. It did not include a contact sheet or supplies of unpublished prints stored for possible use but never issued to the public. Again, ownership of the film when the picture was taken determined authorship and, unless otherwise agreed, the commissioner was the owner of copyright.

The 1956 Act, whilst creating perpetual copyright in unpublished photographs taken on or after June 1 1957, limited copyright protection to 50 years for all photographs (including those subject to Crown copyright) taken before this date. The 1988 Act removed perpetual copyright for all photographs (again, including those subject to Crown copyright) taken from June 1 1957, so photographs made but not published during the period from June 1 1957 to July 31 1989 will remain in copyright until at least midnight on December 31 2039. The EU harmonisation measures which came into effect from January 1 1996 extend the period of protection to 70 years from the end of the year in which the author of the photograph died, provided the author was a national of a Member State of the European Economic Area or the 'country of origin' of the photograph was such a state. Photographs subject to Crown or international organisations copyright are unaffected by this change.

Photographs taken before June 1 1957 receive similar treatment, so duration is now life of the author (or last surviving author) plus 70 years for a national of a Member State of the European Economic Area or a photograph whose 'country of origin' is in an EEA state, provided the work was in copyright in one member state on July 1 1995. If Crown or international organisations copyright applies duration remains 50 years from the end of the year in which made.

No revival takes place for a national of a non-EEA state where the 'country of origin' is also a non-EEA state, but their photographs are protected to the extent they were protected by the author's 'country of origin', again up to a maximum of life plus 70 years or the end of 2039, whichever is the later.

Unpublished photographs by unknown photographers of any date prior to August 1 1989 (Where neither Crown nor international organisations copyright applies) have protection for 70 years from the end of the year in which they were made. If made available to the public during this time the period of protection is either 70 years from the end of year when it was first made available, or the end of 2039, whichever is the later.

Published photographs of any date prior to August 1 1989 by unknown photographers are now protected either for 70 years from the end of the year in which the photograph was made, or 70 years from the end of the year in which it was first made available to the public, or the end of 2039, whichever is the later. Where Crown or international organisations copyright applies, duration is never less than 50 years from the end of the year in which they were published.

Again, for a national of a non-EEA state where the 'country of origin' is also a non-EEA state, protection is that given by their 'country of origin' up to a maximum of life plus 70 years or the end of 2039, whichever is the later.

These changes are due to the principle of equal treatment throughout the Member States of the European Union and the uncertainty over the length of the 'revived' copyright is due to the fact that this is governed by the longest period of protection granted by one of the Member States of the European Economic Area.

Whatever the period of protection a work subject to 'revived' rights can be used by anyone within the EEA without the permission of the copyright owner. Provided a notice of 'intent to use' is served on the copyright owner and the user is prepared to pay a 'reasonable royalty or other remuneration' the owner of a work subject to 'revived' copyright cannot say no to an intended use. What is reasonable in any particular circumstances may be determined by the Copyright Tribunal (administered by The Patent Office) in the absence of agreement between copyright owner and user. Once again this is a matter for specialist legal advice in the light of particular circumstances, especially as, in some cases, 'revived' copyright works may be administered by a collecting society and then the 'reasonable royalty or other remuneration' provisions do not apply. For those needing further details on this now complex area of copyright legislation:

The Copyright Directorate, The Patent Office
25 Southampton Buildings, LONDON WC2A 1AY
(Tel: 020 7438 4777) Website http://www.patent.gov.uk
or
Design and Artists Copyright Society Ltd (DACS)
Parchment House, 13 Northburgh Street, LONDON EC1V 0JP (Tel: 020 7336 8811)

can provide additional information. (See also the 'Existing copies of 'revived' copyright photographs' and 'Limited companies and lapsed organisations' in the section on 'Frequent problems' later in this publication.)

Moral Rights
These are rights which remain with the author of a photograph, irrespective of what happens to the copyright. They were introduced by the 1988 Act and apply to all photographs protected by copyright. They cannot be assigned in the way copyright can be assigned. On the death of someone holding the moral rights which are explained in the following sections, the rights pass to the person the author has nominated in their will. If there is no will, or the will does not mention the subject, the rights are enforceable by the person who inherits the copyright in the photographs or, if the copyright does not form part of the estate, the author's personal representatives. There are three basic rights for photographers and a right of privacy for commissioners of photographs as follows:

Objection to false attribution
This is the right of all photographers (and of anyone else, for that matter) not to have a work falsely attributed to them. It is an automatic right, does not have to be asserted in writing and applies to all photographers whether employed or not and for whatever purpose the work was made. Unlike the other moral rights this one expires 20 years after the death of the photographer. This is one of the reasons photographers should be very careful about bequests. Their heirs should be those that can be trusted to protect their rights. The good reasons for making a will are explained later in this publication and should be read with care.

Safeguarding of privacy in work commissioned for private and domestic purposes
This is a right which belongs to the client and was devised to protect the privacy of those who commissioned the services of a photographer to record weddings, graduation portraits, momentous and personal family gatherings and may also include the recording of medical conditions. The 1988 Act removed copyright in commissioned work from the commissioner and handed it to the photographer, leaving the commissioner exposed to possible publication of private photographs and exploitation by unscrupulous photographers. The photographer now owns the copyright but cannot publish, exhibit or broadcast the photographs without the permission of the commissioner. The photographer may not display prints in a shop window or use them in a portfolio and certainly cannot use them for financial gain should the subject of the photographs become newsworthy. This right does not apply to any photographs taken before August 1 1989.
    (see 'privacy' in the section on 'Frequent problems' later in this publication)

Objection to derogatory treatment of a work (integrity right)

This right allows objection by photographers or their heirs to having their work treated in a manner which amounts to distortion or mutilation or is otherwise damaging to their 'honour or reputation'. Such distortion or mutilation could include manual or digital manipulation, cropping, masking, colorisation, 'comping' (assembly into a composite image), morphing, retouching - anything in fact from moving an inconveniently placed Pyramid to distorting the anatomy of a normally endowed model to ensure that she looks like every other Page 3 girl. If the result is damaging to the reputation of the author, an objection may be lodged. This is an automatic right and there is no need to assert it in order to acquire the right. This right is not generally available to employed photographers except in particular circumstances. Nor does the right to object apply to photographs taken for reporting current events, or, in most cases, for publication in newspapers or magazines or for use in collective reference works such as encyclopaedias. The right does not apply to 'anything done for the purpose of avoiding the commission of an offence'. This could include offences under prohibited sexual activity, indecency, obscenity, race relations, data or child protection, judicial proceedings, official secrecy, public order or emergency powers legislation.

Authorship acknowledgement (paternity right)

The creator of a photographic image now has what has been called the 'paternity' right to have a reasonably prominent credit whenever a work is commercially published, exhibited in public, broadcast, or included in a film shown in public or issued to the public. **This is not an automatic right and must be asserted in writing.**

If the assertion is included in a document assigning copyright to someone else, the right can be enforced against that person and anyone else to whom the copyright is subsequently assigned or licensed. If the assertion is in some other document, in a letter for instance, signed by the author, the right can only be enforced against those who have been notified. Paperwork and photographs rarely stay together and it may be difficult to assert rights if photographs and documents are in the hands of someone with no brief to keep them together. When photographs are published in a book, it is advisable to have a notice that these rights have been asserted by the photographer along with the other copyright details so giving protection to the interests of all concerned. Where the photographer is identified on prints, mounts, frames or anything else to which photographs are attached, the right to a credit will generally apply whenever photographs are exhibited in public, whether or not the identification is still present or visible.

The right does not generally apply to employees for work done in the course of their employment, although again there are exceptions to this. Nor, oddly enough, does it apply to photographs taken for the purposes of reporting current events or, in most cases, for publication in newspapers, magazines or periodicals, or in collective reference works. However, it has always been the general practice, often provided for by contract, for acknowledgements to be given in editorial contexts and the practice still continues. This will generally give photographers contractual rights even if they have no moral right to a credit. Most publications are content to credit their contributing photographers. It ensures a ready supply of material from sources who might be reluctant to cooperate without a printed acknowledgement and such acknowledgements can enhance the reputation of the publication.

Anyone acting on behalf of a photographer such as an agent, picture library, archive or museum, should ensure that the author's assertion of 'paternity' rights is notified to all potential users of the photographer's material. The photographer might be able to sue for negligence if there was a failure to take steps to get this right observed by users.

Publication right

This new right came into effect on December 1 1996. It is a new property right equivalent to copyright which gives protection for 25 years from the end of the year of publication to the individual or legal person who publishes a photograph which has never been previously published, whose copyright has expired and whose copyright was not Crown or Parliamentary copyright. The right only applies if the publisher, (or at least one of them, in the case of a joint publication) is a national of an EEA state and first publication also takes place within the EEA. The right only comes into being if the owner of the physical object, be it negative or print, etc, agrees to the publication. The right works in the same way as normal copyright. Publication is defined as including any communication to the public, not merely issuing copies to the public.

Database right

This is another new right effective from January 1 1998, comparable to copyright, which is designed to protect investment in the selection, collection and assembly of the contents of a database which may be in electronic or manual form. The right, which belongs in the first instance to the maker of the database, is intended to protect against substantial extraction or reutilisation of data and gives protection for 15 years from the end of the year in which the database is made. This right is in addition to any copyright in the contents of the database as an original work and is intended to protect 'sweat of the brow' undertakings of 'works, data or other material' which are 'arranged in a systematic or methodical way' like compilations of the works of particular photographers organised by stylistic features or topic; electronic catalogues of out of copyright photography, etc. Quite how this right will work in practice remains to be seen. As with copyright, database right is subject to general and non-commercial educational and research copying exceptions and fair dealing or 'fair practice'. The right only arises if the maker of the database is a person, real or 'legal' who satisfies EEA nationality requirements.

commissioner) and will be available to lodge with an agency, thus creating welcome additional income. It should be noted however that the original use must have expired or be so limited that it will not overlap in any way the uses to which the agency may wish to put the photographs. It would be good practice to discuss further uses of the material with the commissioner who may have no objections at all but in fairness to the original client, if it would cause problems, don't do it. Remember also that there may be third party rights involved - models, trade marks, etc. When the agreed time period has expired, insist that the client returns the originals in good condition. This has always been normal practice for illustrators and will ensure that, at the very least, a record of work is available for promotional and portfolio purposes as well as being a possible basis of further income. On retirement, or if disaster strikes and ill-health makes further work difficult or impossible, a sizeable collection of pictures will be available which may by then be of historic value and could well represent a substantial part of a pension.

After the death of a copyright owner, the heirs, whoever they may be, will be able to benefit financially for another 70 years. Copyright should be considered as part of a legacy, but be careful. When making a will, bequeath copyright to someone who will be able to manage it intelligently. This may not be the same person to whom house, family silver or the contents of the piggy-bank have been bequeathed and it should be someone who wants it and will not consider it a tedious burden. Remember also that all of the moral rights except objection to false attribution (which lasts only for 20 years after death) are enforceable after one's death for the same length of time as copyright.

Explaining it to clients

There will be times when clients may appear to be justified in insisting that the copyright be assigned to them. A pack shot where only their clearly recognisable, protected product design is featured is a case in point. There will also be times when a job simply will not materialise without a signature on the dotted line, assigning copyright. It is still essential every time to make the point that owning copyright is important and that it is the right of every commissioned photographer to retain it. Point out that maintaining control over the uses not required may result in a more competitive day or shot rate than if they want to buy all imaginable usage rights.

If the client later finds that the pictures are such a success that they want to do something more with them, agree a fee for further use. If they want to syndicate them, agree a percentage of sales. If they are worried that rival companies may later have access to work they have commissioned, agree not to sell anything to any client they care to name. If they want absolute exclusivity for a certain amount of time, agree to an embargo period, known as an exclusivity clause.

It is strongly advisable to get all these kind of things in writing so that there is a good chance that everyone will understand what is being agreed. It is possible to grant a client an exclusive licence for every form of reproduction known till the end of the rights expiry period and for all territories - and still retain copyright, thus keeping a degree of control over unanticipated forms of future exploitation. However, if this kind of licence agreement is considered, it is advisable to get good legal advice first if there is to be any hope at all of such an agreement holding good in the future.

Ownership of material

It is the usual practice in the UK for a fee to be charged for work done on commission plus expenses for film stock and processing. The client might assume that materials reimbursed in this way automatically belongs to them. It's therefore advisable to agree a position on this at the outset and to include a statement of the photographer's ownership of the materials in further licensing on their behalf. Photographers should retain copyright but allow client or agent specific rights to reproduce the work.

Where rights are sold directly to a client these are usually based on considerations of the uses the client wants for the work, where (geographically) it will be used and for how long. The licence is priced accordingly and granting of the licence can be dependent upon payment being made within a reasonable time, or before the work is used. The client will be unable to use the material for anything other than the purposes originally agreed, within the agreed geographical area and for the agreed time period. If the client wants to extend the usage, this can be negotiated, for an extra fee. Whatever the licence its terms must be clearly defined. It is essential to ensure that clients who request exclusivity are aware of the limits of their rights and are not left with the impression that they have bought the image outright. An exclusive licence which is in writing and signed by or on behalf of the copyright owner gives the client the right to sue third parties for copyright infringement, a right they would otherwise have only if copyright had been assigned. The proper way to ensure prompt payment is to state at the outset verbally, on quotations, or on the licence, that the licence will only come into effect when payment has been received and that if any use of the material is made before that time, it will be an infringement of copyright. This could ensure prompt payment, can make all the difference where an advertising agency, for example, is unable to pay the photographer, but the advertiser still wants to use the work and may also short-circuit any arguments based on an implied licence to use material by virtue of a commission.

Remember, copyright is a property right just like owning a house. The freehold can be sold outright or leases on part or parts or all of the property can be negotiated for varying periods of time.

Why copyright should be retained

Holding onto copyright provides both a sword and a shield. A sword, in that the rights owner can benefit financially by licensing further uses of the photographs to other parties; and a shield that can be used as a defence against the use of work in ways that were not agreed and paid for.

Assuming that copyright has not been assigned and a limited licence to use has been issued, dependent upon payment within a reasonable period, there are several advantages:

If the commissioning client gets into financial difficulties and doesn't pay, permission can be refused for any further use of the photographs. If the material has been passed on to a third party - an advertising agency's client for instance or the publisher of a book - it may be possible to claim payment direct from them, even if the third party has already paid the commissioning client.

If the client undertakes additional uses, reproduces the work in territories other than those agreed or outside the agreed time period, it will be possible to claim that copyright has been retained and any unauthorised use will be an infringement. Further fees can be recovered or additional uses prevented. Additionally, if the client goes into liquidation or is wound up, the licence will automatically revert to the copyright owner.

Retention of copyright provides an opportunity to use photographs in a portfolio or for exhibitions or publications of work. There will be no need to go begging to clients for permission, with the possibility of refusal. The copyright owner has a clear legal right of access to the material and will not have to rely on arguments about trade practice and implied rights. It may eventually be possible to offer the work to picture agencies. All libraries and agencies require complete copyright clearance for photographs and to date many photographers have been unable to give this. Now, after the original licensed use has expired, the copyright will be clear (subject to any prior agreement to the contrary with the

Other permitted acts

Educational use
It is not an infringement of copyright to copy a work in the course of instruction or preparation for instruction, provided the copy is not made by a reprographic process and is made by the person giving or receiving instruction. The 1988 Act defines 'reprographic process' as a process for making 'facsimile copies' (including reduced or enlarged copies) or involving the use of an appliance for making multiple copies. No photocopying or copy photography is allowed. It is permitted to copy onto a chalkboard, but not to make photocopies. It seems probable that this section was written with the express intention of encouraging licensing schemes which would provide some economic return to rights owners and indeed, such schemes are in place, notably from the Design and Artists Copyright Society.

Multiple copying by anyone, by any method, for the purposes of setting or answering examination questions, is permitted and no identification of the rights owner or source is required although it is common practice to do so. The Act does not require rights owners to supply an image for examination purposes but where an image is held by someone who intends to use it for setting or answering examination questions they may copy it even if the material is exclusive or rare unless there are contract terms or confidential conditions of supply to prevent this.

Copies made for educational use may not be used for any other purpose.

Library, archive and museum services - research or private study
There are detailed rules for libraries, archives (and museums with these services) which are 'not conducted for a profit' to enable them to copy material for research or private study upon request. Only one copy per person can be made and that copy may not be used for any other purpose. It is advisable to consult the wording of these rules to see if they apply to you.

Library, archive and museum services - conservation work
Libraries, archives (and museums with these) may copy anything in their permanent collection 'in order to preserve or replace it' or 'in order to replace in the permanent collection of another prescribed library or archive an item which has been lost, destroyed or damaged'. It should be noted that these rules do not permit any form of copying, storage and use of photographs or other artistic works appearing in published or unpublished works for use separately from these items. In other words it is not within the scope of the rules to strip out and use separately for loan or consultation, copies of any of the photographs or other artistic works in a book, magazine or other document! 'Prescribed' generally means a non-profit- making organisation. Again, it is advisable to consult the wording of the rules to see if your organisation or service comes within the scope of this provision.

Advertising a work for sale
It is not an infringement of copyright to issue photographs of an artistic work to the public to advertise it for sale, but these photographs may not be used for any other purpose

without the permission of the copyright owner. Such purposes would include continued sales of a catalogue of works after an auction or a sale is completed.

Works on public display
Sculptures, models for buildings and works of artistic craftsmanship (such as stained glass), if permanently situated in a public place, or in premises open to the public and buildings (which includes bridges) may be freely photographed, though in fairness to the sculptor, architect, designer, engineer or artist and in the interests of researchers in the future, captions should identify them where appropriate. In some cases a credit may be required if the artist's moral rights have been asserted. It should be noted that photographs on public display are not covered by this exception so photography of photographs, on say headstones in a graveyard is not permitted without the consent of the copyright owner. Works which are on private property but are visible from public places, continue to enjoy full rights protection. This can constitute a problem when the work is in a private garden and is clearly visible from a public right of way. If the work is permanently displayed in a public place, there are no restrictions on photography. But a private garden, unless it is opened to the public, is not a public place and the Act will apply. The work should not be photographed for publication unless its inclusion in the photograph is 'incidental'. (See the section on 'incidental inclusion' below).

Trespassing upon private property to take photographs without asking permission, can lead to an action for trespass but the photographs taken remain the copyright property of the photographer, who is not generally under any obligation to hand them over if caught. 'Trespassers Will Be Prosecuted' is usually an empty threat since trespass is only a criminal offence in special circumstances. The owners of premises open to the public may make a charge for entry or place prohibitions on photography as a condition of entry. These prohibitions could be printed on the ticket, be displayed on a board by the gates or be published in membership literature in the case of premises offering season tickets. Photographs taken despite the restrictions will nevertheless remain the copyright property of the photographer but the photographer will be liable to be sued under contract law if they are subsequently published or otherwise exploited for economic gain. In some cases publication of photographs will be prevented under the laws of confidence.

Incidental inclusion
Copyright in a photograph is not now infringed when it is incidentally included in another photograph, artistic work, film, or broadcast. Equally, photographers are not in breach of copyright if they include other people's copyright material in their own work without permission, provided its inclusion is only incidental.

Inclusion of a copyright work would not normally be regarded as incidental if it is a deliberate or an important feature of the exercise. There is no definition of 'incidental' and the legal position may not be clear cut. However a basic guideline can be applied. Imagine a photograph of a person in front of a well known, copyright photographic print. The inclusion of the print in the background is unlikely to be incidental unless it quite genuinely just happened to be there. Whether or not the background is in focus and the size of the print in relation to the whole picture will also be relevant. If in doubt, it is usually better to err on the safe side since getting it wrong could be costly!

Public administration
No permission is required for various uses of copyright works in relation to the following:

- **Parliamentary and judicial proceedings**
- **Royal Commissions and Statutory Inquiries**
- **Material communicated to the Crown in the course of public business**
- **Public Records**

Most of these activities speak for themselves. However, if use is made of copyright material for gain, or for purposes other than that for which it was originally required, it is possible to seek redress.

It is also possible to seek anonymity in these contexts, which, in some cases, may be essential to protect a photographer from the wrath of those who have faced prosecution because photographs have been used as evidence.

Compliance costs

This book is intended to give general guidance on the do's and don'ts of copyright law, and how to comply with this. Under all circumstances the law does not expect an intending user of a photograph to spend a disproportionate amount of time and money on tracing a possible rights owner. There has to be a balance between the expected economic gain of using a work and the cost of tracing the rights owner. If, as a minimum, an intending user keeps a record of all enquiries made to trace an owner, makes enquiries of appropriate sources, possibly advertises in a relevant newspaper or periodical and sets money aside which reasonably reflects the amount a rights owner might expect to gain from the use of their work, then they may be seen to have done everything they reasonably could. Such actions will be taken into account if there is any dispute over a use which is serious enough to go before the Copyright Tribunal or any other court. However, as a matter of law, the copyright owner of a work normally has the final say on usage and if they do not agree to this they may be able to insist on the withdrawal or destruction of unauthorised copies.

Trading under the new copyright legislation

Photographers, their agents, and their clients should balance their claims to copyright against their own needs and legitimate use by others. Agreements should grant a licence to carry out the full purpose of the agreement and should also recognise the freedom of the photographer to do things that are not prejudicial to the purpose of those agreements. In other words, a mutually beneficial relationship must be achieved.

Assignments and licences

Some clients who deal directly with photographers insist on retaining full control of all rights as they did before August 1 1989. They can seek to achieve this in two ways; either by requiring the photographer to sign a full assignment of copyright or, increasingly, by means of a 'grant-back licence'. An assignment of copyright is a legally binding document which may transfer all or selected rights from the photographer to someone else, could be hidden within the many clauses in small print on the back of an art order and may be worded in such a way that it becomes a one-time agreement covering everything the photographer does for the client for the rest of what could be a long working life. It might not be binding but this would be for the courts to decide, would take a long time and cost a great deal of money - all of which could be avoided by reading the small print first. Every order should be carefully studied to ensure that there are no such clauses included.

The BPLC advises photographers to think very carefully before signing or agreeing to a full assignment of copyright. Control of material will be lost if such an assignment is signed before payment is received. Major bargaining counters will be lost. If the client later extends the use of the material beyond the original brief, no legal claim for extra payment can be made, unless specifically agreed. Clients will own the material and can do precisely what they want with it, including licensing it on to a third party or re-assigning copyright. The client will have no obligation towards the photographer who will have no legal right to any further payments. Nothing remains but the moral rights.

And thereby hangs a tale. Amongst the acknowledgements in the first edition of this publication, and indeed in this new edition, was 'Demis Roussos -for his continuing inspiration'. This has caused endless speculation. In fact the reason is simple. Some years ago, a photographer photographed Demis Roussos, who was attired in a splendid smoking jacket. The work was commissioned, it was before the 1988 Act and the photographer was not in a position to retain copyright. Shortly afterwards, Demis Roussos was involved in a spectacular hi-jacking. The commissioners cashed in and sold the pictures worldwide. The photographer got nothing. He was converted and became heavily involved in the production of the first edition of this book. Demis Roussos continues to be an inspiration!

A more sophisticated way of doing things is for the client to insist on an exclusive licence in existing work, together with an assignment of copyright in future work yet to be created, which simultaneously agrees to licence back to the photographer all the rights the client doesn't want since this gives the client the right to sue an infringer. This 'grant-back licence' can appear attractive, but it puts the client firmly in control of usage and if the rights the client doesn't want are only vaguely specified or are listed too restrictively the photographer will have serious problems in exploiting work effectively. All photographers should be aware of the need to license their material correctly, be it direct to a client or to an agent for

Fair Dealing or Fair Practice

Fair Dealing (increasingly nowadays referred to as 'Fair Practice') is a term used to cover copying of protected works without the need to obtain permission from the rights owners or to make payment to them. It is limited to several particular purposes, as follows.

Research or private study
Fair dealing with a photograph for the purposes of research or private study does not infringe copyright in the photograph. There are tight restrictions on multiple copies in this context. Strictly, this includes faxes, digital copies, photocopies and the like, however if these are made in the course of seeking permission to use or are held simply for reference by an individual without intent to gain a financial benefit there is unlikely to be objection from rights holders. If such 'fair practice' copies, especially in electronic form, are tagged or clearly marked as such rights holders are also unlikely to object.

Criticism and review
Reproduction of a photograph is allowed for the purpose of criticism or review of the photograph itself, or some other work, provided that it is accompanied by a credit identifying authorship and the title of the work, if any. Again, this must be for genuine fair practice purposes and not just for decoration, to fill an empty space on a page or to provide an educational resource.

Reporting current events
The 1988 Act recognised reporting current events as an activity which may require the use of copyright material. However, the UK Parliament was persuaded that the living of news photographers and photo-journalists would be seriously affected if copyright photographs could be used without payment and the action defended as fair practice. Photographs are specifically excepted from this fair dealing sub-section and may not be used in this context without the permission of the rights owner. This is contrary to practice in some other EEA states and this important provision may yet be eroded by yet more proposals under consideration in the European Parliament.

Infringements

The rule of law says 'Ignorance of the law is no excuse for failure to obey'. Infringement of the civil law may take place in many ways ie: Copying or replication, broadcasting, false attribution, breach of privacy, derogatory treatment, omission of credits where the right has been asserted. Additionally, it can be a criminal offence to possess an infringing item in the course of business or to possess the means to make an infringing item or the apparatus to show or receive an infringing item. It can be an offence to copy a slide or transparency commercially on the grounds that it would be convenient to do so and will prevent the need to contact the photographer every time the photograph is required. Ignorance of the law is no defence to a criminal prosecution if the infringing party has reason to believe an infringement is taking place. An employee cannot be expected or required by an employer to commit an illegal act, but equally an employee, or anyone else, for that matter who regularly deals with copyright material should be aware of the law for themselves since they can be held personally accountable for their actions; especially in situations where an employer or client denies any corporate wrongdoing!

Copying improperly

The 1988 Act defines copying in relation to photography as 'reproducing the work in any material form', including 'storing the work in any medium by electronic means'. That covers a lot of ground and was designed to include processes that nobody had yet thought of. Rights owners may object - especially in situations where storage and dissemination of images electronically is concerned. UK law allows up to six years from the moment any infringement occurs for the rights owner to seek a legal remedy. If the rights owner was deliberately prevented from knowing that an infringement had occurred, this is fraud and the time limit does not apply. It is best to seek advice promptly, either from your professional association, or a legal advisor, in all but minor cases because attempts to go it alone could inadvertently weaken one's position. For those in doubt, member organisations of the BPLC will usually be able to advise on available legal services.

Copy shops should display notices pointing out that it is not permitted to make copies of anything which is within copyright, but these notices are often difficult to see and frequently covered with other items. No business should ever copy anything, be it a transparency, slide or a print, without first checking on copyright, although usually their own terms and conditions of business make it clear that they copy only on the basis that the person presenting the material for copying has the authority to do so and will bear the responsibility if anything goes wrong. Social photographers are the usual sufferers here. Clients have been known to evade the cost of multiple prints from the copyright owner by taking a proof to a cheap copy shop. This is a blatant copyright infringement and should be pursued energetically by all legal means, thus raising media interest, which might deter others from cashing in.

any terms and conditions of business that may be used.

It is difficult to administer rights if the physical property to which they relate is permanently in the hands of a client. It will also be difficult to license rights in photographs to other parties if they are unable to get access to the material. Despite everything, the legal position is that if copyright is retained by the photographer, the owner of the photographs must generally allow access to the material to enable the copyright owner to exercise legitimate rights. However, as clients may lose, damage or destroy the original material, parting with it is not recommended!

Supplying stock photographs

Never submit stock photographs to a prospective client without using a delivery note detailing the number of photographs supplied, a reference number for each item and a brief descriptive caption. Delivery notes with clearly written terms and conditions printed on the back are available from the Association of Photographers and from BAPLA, the NUJ and BIPP. Always ensure that a credit line or name and a means of contact are on every photograph and on the mount of every transparency.

The rights conferred to reproduce photographs are called 'reproduction rights'. For a mutually agreed fee a licence is granted to reproduce for a specified purpose, in a specified territory and for a specified period of time. The granting of such a licence does not involve the assignment of copyright. When licensing reproduction rights, it is essential to ensure that conflicting rights are not licensed to two or more clients at the same time and that restrictions imposed by, or agreed with, the original commissioner are observed. Models may place certain restrictions on use. They may prefer not to appear in tobacco promotion or advertising for furs. Not only should their wishes be respected but you may also be sued for breach of contract if you ignore any agreement reached with them.

Remember, copyright is not assigned, moral rights are not waived and photographs are not sold when reproduction rights in stock photographs are licensed.

Licensing reproduction rights

When a licence is granted, the following types of question should be asked in order to provide a basis for calculating the fee:

• Who exactly is requesting the licence?

• How will the photograph be reproduced or shown and at what size will it appear?

• For what purpose will the work be reproduced?

• Over what time period will the work be available?

• What is the print run?

• In what territories will the work be available?

• How many editions or impressions are intended?

• Will the author of the work be identified?

• Does the client require an exclusivity clause?

• Will the work be used to advertise the final product?

• Will the work be stored electronically?

• Will the work be masked or adapted in any way?

How to protect your work

Under UK law, there is no requirement to take any formal steps (such as depositing a copy or registering anywhere) to establish copyright. It is important though to take certain precautions in order to inform other people of the legal position and it is essential to assert, in writing, the moral right to a credit where applicable.

To help protect work, every photographic print, transparency mount and negative bag (assuming an obligation to supply negatives, which should be resisted if at all possible), should carry the Universal Copyright Convention symbol; © followed by the name of the copyright owner. The wording Copyright, or its official American legal abbreviation 'Copr', may also be helpful, especially if it is intended to operate in North America or the Russian Federation. Strictly, a date should be included if operating in a territory which applies the Universal Copyright Convention rules but is not essential elsewhere. The same principles apply to electronic or digital versions. A reliable, permanent telephone or fax number or e-mail address should ensure that the photographer can be contacted, material returned and payments made.

Adding 'credit required' or similar words will often in practice result in a credit even if it does not amount to a formal assertion of the moral right to be identified.

To prevent confusion, a brief caption is vital. Work submitted to picture libraries and agencies requires a fuller caption which can be provided separately. There is a limit to what can be written on a transparency mount but there should be enough to identify both the image and its orientation, if this is likely to be ambiguous. Whatever is written should always be legible.

Remedies against infringement

Copyright is a property right. The owner, the owner's heirs or anyone to whom copyright has been assigned can take action against someone who has infringed copyright just as action can be taken against a squatter who has invaded private property. If a possible infringement is discovered in advance, an injunction to stop the use may be obtainable. If it's too late, it is possible to sue for damages to compensate for the loss and to apply for an injunction to stop any repetition. Except in minor cases, it is generally advisable to seek legal advice or consult a professional association such as those represented in the BPLC before doing anything alone. The period of time within which action must be taken is generally six years from the date of infringement.

If someone, as a business venture, knowingly pirates or bootlegs copyright work, it is a criminal offence punishable by a fine and/or up to two years in jail. The copyright owner is entitled to appiy for a court order to have all the copies delivered up to him or her and, if that doesn't work, to have them seized. Infringing copies can be seized by the rights owner so long as the local police station is told first, a prescribed notice is served and force isn't used. Although a court order isn't needed for this remedy, it's essential to get legal advice before acting.

Bear in mind that the pirated item may be thousands of books which, whether delivered according to a court order or seized, will have to be stored. Thousands of books are heavy and bulky. Will the floors take the weight? What will it cost to store elsewhere?

It is also worth bearing in mind that the most usual pirated items are posters which are sold in city streets and at car boot sales. Those selling such posters are likely to cut and run if challenged but are usually managed by the unscrupulous who will not take kindly to any efforts to assert rights. It would be a great mistake to tackle them without legal backup. Local Trading Standards Officers may be prepared to help but by the time they have got their act together, the bird is likely to have flown - to a pitch in the next borough. Unfortunately, the police generally think they have better things to do and are unlikely to be helpful without persuasion. They are far more likely to become interested if solitary efforts to assert rights lead to bloodshed - but they may not support the 'right' side.

Frequent problems

In this section we have tried to deal with some of the more frequent questions asked of BPLC members.

Privacy

Owing to the excesses of certain sections of the media and the unscrupulous behaviour of a few photographers and others with an eye for the main chance, privacy has become and remains a hot potato.

It appears likely that eventually greater restrictions will be placed on what can and what cannot be photographed. (The right to privacy in work commissioned for private and domestic purposes is discussed above in the section on moral rights.) At present, the restrictions are generally moral ones. There is no specific legislation in the UK to prevent photographers from taking pictures which infringe privacy. The restrictions lie in the use of the pictures and even then, there are those who will publish and be damned because the extra sales generated may be worth it financially and the chances of getting anything worse than a slapped wrist are unlikely. The law of confidence can sometimes be a powerful weapon, but only in restricted and none too clearly defined circumstances. In the UK, photographs of people taken in the street or in a public place are not restricted by copyright law as to use. However, such pictures could be subject to the laws of libel. It is advisable to establish how pictures like these will be used if supplying from stock or on a commissioned basis. If a client intends to suggest that a percentage of a crowd suffer from a debilitating disease, have unnatural habits or are simply divorced and the crowd is peopled with recognisable faces, they could raise a very expensive objection. What is a crowd? London Bridge at 9 o'clock in the morning is a crowd. So is a room full of people or the start of the London Marathon. Some claim that a crowd is more than half a dozen people, some that the figure should be twelve and others that a crowd has to be hundreds. It is clearly impossible to supply a model release in such circumstances but it is important to realise that objections could be raised and care should be taken when supplying such pictures, particularly for advertising and promotional purposes. There is no UK equivalent to the American rights of privacy and publicity, which restrict exploitation of an individual's likeness for commercial purposes. However, famous people and others may not take kindly to such uses and often take legal action against anyone who tries it. Photographers are bound by law to observe certain rules relating to breaches of trust or confidence when photographing people, especially children.

Photographs of buildings taken from the street or a public place are normally legal but beware of using such photographs for advertising or promotional purposes, or for anything which could be construed as derogatory, without seeking consent from someone with the authority to grant it. It's asking for trouble if for instance, pictures are supplied of a thatched cottage for an insurance promotion and the owner of the cottage has been turned down by the same insurance company. The Advertising Standards Authority in the UK, and now the Press Complaints Commission, increasingly tend to deal with individual privacy issues far more stringently than does the law.

Photographs of buildings, and of sculptures, models for buildings or works of artistic craftsmanship permanently situated in a public place or premises open to the public, do not infringe copyright, but beware of using them for advertising or promotional purposes without consent. It could involve breach of contract if photography is specifically prohibited.

Model Releases

It is advisable to obtain written permission whenever taking photographs of people, whether professional models or not. Certainly, on a commercial shoot, it would be absurd to forget this essential document which will enable the rights owner to make use of the material for the agreed purposes. In advertising, a model release must be available and many picture libraries and agencies will refuse to accept stock without adequate releases. Suitable Model Release forms can be obtained from some BPLC members.

Multiple copyrights in the same artistic work

There is often more than one copyright involved in a photograph. Retouching that substantially changes rather than enhances the photograph, bits of different copyright photographs in a collage, pack shots with a copyright logo etc, all could have justifiable copyright claims. Anyone making use of such an image must ensure that clearance is obtained from these other copyright owners for the initial and all further uses of the finished product.

Retouching

This is an aspect of the law which is shrouded in fog and has all the makings of a lawyers benefit as there are many different views on the issues involved, so beware! If a client has employed a retoucher to work, with the consent of the copyright owner, on a print, duplicate transparency or copy negative that they themselves have had made and the retouching has sufficiently changed the original so that it is substantially a new work, there is dual copyright in the retouched copy and the client has the right to retain it. Copyright in the original work is not affected by the existence of a new copyright in the retouched version. Retouching a copyright work without permission is an infringement and may also breach moral rights. If retouching has been done with consent on an original transparency, negative or print, these items remain the property of the original rights owner who has the right to retain them, although there is again dual copyright in the final image and the permission of the client and the retoucher must be sought before making commercial use of the results. If the retouching was done without the consent of the copyright owner, he or she will have the right to claim for damage to the original and there may be moral rights implications. Retouching an out-of-copyright photograph, again to a sufficient degree so that it is a different image, creates a new copyright in the combined work but does not affect other prints of the original. Copyright in the new image then lasts for 70 years from the end of the year in which the retoucher dies. Exactly the same principles apply to digital or electronic copies.

Copying by implied consent

With the change in the law many organisations, businesses and educational institutions are now taking the tracing and crediting of copyright ownership and authorship in photography a great deal more seriously than they have ever done in the past. However, because of the time, expense and uncertainty involved copyright clearance requests sent to a last known address or care of an organisation that might be able to identify the copyright owner are often phrased in such a way that, if no reply is received within a given time, it will be assumed that consent to the request has been granted and copying for the stated purpose will take place regardless. If the request is reasonable, states the limits of use and offers credits and remuneration, all well and good. If it does not the BPLC advises that an ultimatum of this kind should be rejected in exactly the same way as a demand for a full assignment of copyright and for the same reasons. Whether accepting or rejecting, a response is always advisable because if the work is used in a way which is not acceptable or is not in accordance with the offer, attempts to gain redress may be prejudiced by the user claiming that no response implied full consent to their actions, which is a difficult and expensive argument to refute, especially if lawyers become involved.

If a photograph is issued at some time with no intention to charge for its reproduction, such as for public relations or related purposes, there may be an implied consent for the recipient to copy this and to use it as often as they wish without consulting the copyright owner further as long as the usage is clearly within the original purposes. Reproduction or sale of such photographs for gain in contexts not originally envisaged by the issuer may be outside this implied consent and the copyright owner may have to be consulted in the normal way before any reproduction takes place.

Copyright owners of this kind of material who wish to retain control over usage outside of that initially intended are advised to mark it 'free of fee', briefly describing the conditions under which this applies and prohibit copying after a certain date without prior consent. Once again, if a credit is required whenever such a photograph is reproduced this must be stated and preferably on the print, transparency mount or alongside a digital image, etc.

Existing copies of 'revived' copyright photographs

Obviously photographs that are subject to the new 'revived' copyright provisions whether published or unpublished have been legitimately copied and collected ever since they entered public domain. Even although these are now back in copyright such copies can still be used within the EEA without the consent of the rights owner or the need to serve notice of 'intent to use' provided it can be shown the copies were in existence, or that arrangements had been made to issue copies to the public, prior to January 1 1996.

Limited companies and lapsed organisations

The EU harmonisation measures creating 'revived' copyright give the problem of tracing ownership of the new rights in order, at the very least, to serve the notice of 'intent to use'; a task which is particularly complicated for unpublished photographs of uncertain date in this category because so many of them were routinely taken by unidentified photographers and the rights were owned by companies and organisations that have ceased to trade or been wound up long ago. There is no simple answer to this problem. The options are to make routine checks with the Archives Section of the UK Companies House and also the Public Record Office, or with the resources of British Library to show that a UK based company or organisation really is defunct and that there appears to be nobody to claim the rights. Enquiry of The Copyright Office at Her Majesty's Stationery Office or the Treasury Solicitors may also be advisable. A record kept of this kind of enquiry is vital in case someone subsequently comes forward to claim the rights and the issue is important enough to argue before a court. Also, always remember when it is reasonable to assume the author of a photograph died 70 or more calendar years ago and 'it is not possible by reasonable enquiry to ascertain the identity of the author' that copyright expiry can be assumed. Most photographs carry inherent clues as to their probable date of exposure so a little bit of commonsense in the interpretation of the image may save an awful lot of trouble!

What can't be done

There are usually stringent restrictions on photography in theatres, auditoria and concert halls, etc. The rights of the performers could be infringed by filming or making a video of substantial parts of a performance. The copyright in still photography taken at such venues will belong to the photographer, or their employer, whatever the restrictions but commercial use will be in breach of contract. The contract could be the terms and conditions printed on the back of the ticket or a document which photographers might be required to sign before they are allowed on the premises. It could also be part of an annual membership subscription. Remember also that surreptitious entry to an event or a property could expose the intruder to an action for trespass and that, although copyright in any photographs taken would belong to the photographer who took them, however entry was achieved, making any commercial use of the results might not be lawful. Photographing or copying individual frames from a film infringes the copyright in the film. A television broadcast can be photographed but only for private and domestic purposes.

It is permitted to refer to a copyright work for artist's reference, so long as the final work does not reproduce 'any substantial part' of the original. If the result is recognisable as having been derived from the original source, the second work may be liable for a fee or damages which could be substantial, according to what use has been made of the derivative work.

What constitutes 'any substantial part' has not been clearly defined. There have been countless legal decisions on individual cases, but although some general principles have been laid down, there is often room for argument. The Oxford English Dictionary, in amongst a mass of obscure references to Middle English, lists one clear definition. 'Of ample or considerable amount, quantity, or dimensions'. The BPLC are indebted to Geoffrey Adams for his intelligent and witty definition: "Each instance must be examined in the light of the particular circumstances but the courts have made it clear that it's the quality of the extract that counts, not the quantity. A relatively small extract could be regarded as substantial if it expressed the essence of the whole photograph. Thus the lips of Marilyn Monroe extracted from a head to toe photograph constitute 'a substantial amount'."

It is illegal to take photographs in any court of law everywhere in the UK, except Scotland. Even there, it may be done only with the permission of the court authorities and such permission has never been given! Remember also that a court of law is a process not just a place, so the prohibition applies when a judge and jury go out to inspect or view something in connection with a case being tried. Any photographs that have ever appeared, other than occasional pictures of the murderer Crippen in the dock which were taken in the 1920s before the law changed, are set-up pictures taken during training sessions for court officials and the like - or illegal! (It is also, incidentally, illegal to draw in court and those court drawings which appear on television are produced by a very small group of artists who are obliged to work from memory in the corridors outside the courtrooms.) It is also forbidden to take photographs in the Houses of Parliament without permission from the authorities there. There are many other restrictions too from post offices to police stations, prisons and other government buildings, especially those related to the defence of the UK. Photography in hospitals or schools is not normally allowed except with permission from the authorities responsible for running these places.

Bank notes, coins and postage stamps are not only protected by copyright, they also have their own special laws and regulations relating to protection from fraud or forgery as do such things as the Royal Arms and Insignia, etc. For guidance on these, the contact points are:

Bank notes
Principal, Issue Office, Bank of England, LONDON EC2R 8AH (Tel: 020 7601 4028)

Coinage
Debt and Reserves Management Team, HM Treasury, Parliament Street, LONDON SW1P 3AG (Tel: 020 7270 1832)

Postage stamps
Manager of Special Stamps, Royal Mail, Royal London House, 22-25 Finsbury Square, LONDON EC2A 1NL (Tel: 020 7614 7013)

Further guidance on the reproduction of postage stamps and bank notes generally may also be obtained from:

The British Library, Philatelic Collections, Great Russell Street, LONDON WC1B 3DG (Tel: 020 7412 7635)

For guidance on reproduction of Royal Arms and Insignia contact: Lord Chamberlain's Office, Buckingham Palace, LONDON SW1A 1AA (Tel: 020 7930 4832)

Maps and charts in whatever form are, of course, also protected by copyright. In the UK such items, where produced on official authority have their copyright administered by the Ordnance Survey, British Geological Survey, the Civil Aviation Authority or the United Kingdom Hydrographic Office. For guidance on these items, the contact points are:

Mapping
Copyright Branch, Ordnance Survey, Romsey Road, Maybush, SOUTHAMPTON S016 4GU (Tel: 023 80 792227/6)

Copyright Branch, Ordnance Survey of Northern Ireland
Colby House, Stranmills Court, BELFAST BT9 5BJ (Tel: 02890 255755)

British Geological Survey
Kingsley Dunham Centre, Keyworth, NOTTINGHAM NG12 5GG (Tel: 0115 936 3100)

Charting
Head of Aeronautical Charts and Graphic Arts Section, Civil Aviation Authority, CAA House, 45-59 Kingsway, LONDON WC2B 6TE (Tel: 020 7832 5563/5566)

Copyright Section, The United Kingdom Hydrographic Office, TAUNTON TA1 2DN (Tel: 01823 337900 ext 4248/3454/3644/4194)

For guidance on Crown copyright matters generally contact:

The Copyright Office, Her Majesty's Stationery Office, St Clements House, 2-16 Colegate, NORWICH NR3 1BQ (Tel: 01603 621 0000)

Remember also that typefaces and typographical arrangement (ie, the design, layout and typeface of a page) are protected by copyright and that whilst use of a typeface in the ordinary course of typing, printing, etc, is not an infringement of copyright, reproducing a photograph of a font, or a 'typographical arrangement' without the consent of the copyright owner is, unless such use is in the context of 'fair dealing' or 'fair practice'.

Making a will

You do not need a lawyer to make a will covering simple needs. Even a dated scrap of signed paper with basic instructions and the signatures of witnesses with addresses could ensure that property is distributed as wished. But a professionally written will, regularly updated to take into consideration changes in circumstances and in the law, is infinitely preferable.

A photographer has assets other than a house and goods and chattels. Copyright is an intellectual property and can be bequeathed in the same way as anything else. Photographers can choose who they want to exercise their moral rights after their death. Photographers should ensure that when it comes to drawing up a will, a solicitor is used who is professionally aware of the intellectual property rights involved and these rights should be treated as a separate entity. Spouses or partners may not necessarily be the ideal persons to handle the complexities of copyright and moral rights and should be consulted about this. The future recipient of any intellectual property should be asked. They may not want it!

Copyright outside the United Kingdom

Of course, nothing is ever easy. This book refers to the UK only. Other countries have different laws and these laws apply if, for instance, a German publisher wishes to use material supplied by a British photographer in Germany. The European Union have decreed that the term of copyright throughout EU Member States will be harmonised at 70 years after the author's death which required legislation in every member country and has produced some startling effects, especially where the 'author' is a 'legal person' such as a company or organisation. Further afield, the USA has also gone over to the same basic rule, scrapped registration of copyright as a prerequisite of protection and also restored protection to works in the public domain. The reader will need to verify the exact position as and when the need arises since it is not possible to give all the specific detail required in a work of general guidance such as this, particularly as laws are constantly changing.

It doesn't help that there are countries which consider photography should be subject to an 'artistic merit test'. Thus, a photographic study which could be considered an artistic work may win many more years' copyright protection than a documentary photograph and even more than a 'simple' photograph which could be anything from a snapshot of a cat to a grabbed picture in the street. In the UK, every picture is given the same protection, be it an outrageous, over-the-top confection for a worldwide calendar or a snapshot taken by a child. In Germany, a spectacular, prize-winning documentary photograph may cease to be protected during the lifetime of the photographer whilst a lily, tastefully arranged in a vase against drapes, could continue to provide an income for 70 years after the photographer's death. A photograph could be considered a 'photographic work' in one country and not in another and could be exploited by a third party without the rights owner being paid.

Attitudes towards moral rights differ across Europe and the re-write of copyright laws to harmonise this will be difficult. There is no intention to create one law for all of Europe but there is an intention to harmonise the term of protection. This brings in new problems, as has been indicated throughout this book, especially in relation to 'revived' copyright.

As at June 1999, when this publication was completed, the duration of copyright for photographs in Europe, North America and a selection of countries of interest to the readership of this work was as shown below. Please note the periods and artistic merit tests shown for EU countries are those that applied to photographs immediately before the harmonisation directive was implemented. *A † shows which countries have actually written the life plus 70 year rule into their national law.* This approach has been adopted because it is not possible, in a work of this kind, to show all the complexity of the transitional provisions in each country and how they have dealt with the problem of protecting photographs for a fixed period when they may also have an artistic merit test. Further specialist advice will be needed for most practical purposes, but as a general rule it is fair to say that in all cases the longest applicable term of protection is still in force.

Australia

Photographic works: 50 years from year-end of making or publication.
Photographic works in Crown copyright: 50 years from year-end of making or publication.

Austria†

Photographic works: 70 years *post mortem auctoris** (pma).
Simple photographs: 30 years from year-end of making or publication.

Belgium†
Photographic works: 50 years pma + 10 years war-time extension.

Canada
Photographic works: 50 years from year-end of making.
Photographic works in Crown copyright: 50 years from year-end of making or publication.

Denmark†
Photographic works: 25 years from year-end of making.

Finland†
Photographic works: 50 years from year-end of making.

France†
Photographic works: 50 years pma + 14 years and 274 days for works still protected on August 13 1941 (war-time extension); plus possible additional 30 years for 'death whilst serving France'.

Germany†
Photographic works: 70 years pma.
Documentary works: 50 years from year-end of publication or 50 years from year-end of making if unpublished within these 50 years.
Simple photographs: 25 years from year-end of publication or 25 years from year-end of making if unpublished within these 25 years.

Greece†
Photographic works: 50 years pma.
Simple photographs: 10 years from year-end of publication for reproductions in anthologies.

Ireland†
Photographic works: 50 years pma or 50 years from year-end of publication.
Photographic works in Government copyright: 50 years from year-end of publication.

Italy†
Photographic works: 50 years from year-end of making + 6 years war-time extension.
Simple photographs: 20 years from year-end of making.

Japan
Photographic works: 50 years from year-end of making or publication + 10 years extension for citizens of France, UK and US.

Luxembourg†
Photographic works: 50 years from year-end of making.

Netherlands†
Photographic works: 50 years pma.

New Zealand
Photographic works: 50 years pma.
Computer-generated works: 50 years from year-end of making.
Photographic works in Crown copyright: 50 years from year-end of making.

Norway
Photographic works: 15 years pma, 25 years from year-end of first publication in the case of corporate bodies.

Portugal†
Photographic works 25 years from year-end of making.

Russian Federation
Photographic works: 50 years pma, 50 years from year-end of publication if published as an anonymous work.

Spain†
Photographic works: 60 years pma.
Simple photographs: 25 years from year-end of making.

Sweden†

Photographic works: 50 years pma for artistic and scientific photographs, all others 25 years from year-end of making.

Switzerland

Photographic works: 70 years pma.

United States of America

Photographic works: 70 years pma or December 31 2002, whichever is the later, for works created after January 1 1978. Works created but not published or registered before January 1 1978 have 95 years of protection from the date that copyright was originally secured.

95 years from year-end of publication in the case of anonymous or pseudonymous works or 120 years from year of creation, whichever expires first.

*pma (Post mortem auctoris): *after the author's death*

Conclusion

When the 'ABC' was begun, the aim was to keep it as simple as possible and to eliminate words or phrases liable to confuse or which required the reader to reach for a dictionary. The complexities of copyright legislation in a European and global context are such that in this edition it has became increasingly difficult to do this without leaving out essential items and it has again been occasionally necessary to supply a rather convoluted explanation to circumnavigate some legal phrase that required too much thinking about! However, if readers have understood the contents of this book and act according to the advice supplied, they are less likely to find themselves in difficulties with copyright and related rights and will know what to do if trouble looms. Copyright can be a fascinating subject with endless opportunities for debate. There will always be someone who will say 'but what if...' at the moment when it all seems to be coming out right. A good working knowledge of copyright will ensure that when it comes to debate, the result will benefit the copyright owner and thus, all copyright owners. Debate can be education at its best but it's necessary to know the facts. The facts of copyright keep evolving to keep abreast with the pace of change in the world so be aware of this and keep a look out for the next edition of this book!